Families

by Gloria Johns

PEARSON

Scott Foresman

Editorial Offices: Glenview, Illinois • Parsippany, New Jersey • New York, New York
Sales Offices: Boston, Massachusetts • Duluth, Georgia • Glenview, Illinois
Coppell, Texas • Sacramento, California • Mesa, Arizona

The family cooks.

The family cleans.

The family rakes.

The family shops.

The family walks.

The family plays.

The family reads.